pressure
cooking

THE AUSTRALIAN
Women's Weekly

CONTENTS

AUSTRALIAN CUP AND SPOON MEASUREMENTS ARE METRIC. A CONVERSION CHART APPEARS ON PAGE 77.

It seems to me that cooks fall into two categories: those who use and love appliances and those who don't. I fall into the "don't" category. But, after experimenting with the smallest-available stove-top pressure cooker at home and tasting all the wonderful recipes for this book, I have been converted.

Pamela Clark
Food Director

THE PRESSURE COOKER

Pressure-cooked food is full of concentrated flavours; after all, there is no evaporation taking place during cooking time. The natural moisture that comes from the food can't go anywhere but back into the liquid in the cooker – which becomes the sauce – and the essence of the food itself.

Pressure cooking is economical in terms of the use of fuel, as about two-thirds of the conventionally-cooked food's cooking time simply vanishes; this saves time, energy, money and of course keeps the kitchen cooler. The fact is, the food, the liquid and the resulting steam that are sealed within the pressure cooker during the cooking time reach a very high temperature – higher than normal – which softens the fibres in the food, resulting in flavoursome, tender food.

Also, pressure cookers do wonders with the cheaper cuts of meat; tough meat is tenderised in no time at all. Ask the butcher what meat he has that's suitable for stewing or braising – you'll be surprised how inexpensive these cuts are.

Pulses of all types – dried beans, peas, lentils and soy beans – tenderise quickly in the pressure cooker, even without soaking beforehand.

The pressure cookers of today – both stove-top and electric – are completely safe and easy to use; their pressure regulators are much more refined than those used on the cookers of yesteryear. Read the instruction manual carefully before you start. Like most appliances, they all have slightly different features.

Both types of cookers, stove- and bench-top, work in the same way; the main difference is in the control of the appliance. The stove-top cooker needs the cook to control the pressure by adjusting the heat source at the appropriate time, whereas the bench-top cooker does this work for you – it controls and adjusts the pressure. There is not a huge difference in price between the two types.

Both cookers are quite large and bulky to store, the bench-top cooker of a similar capacity to a stove-top cooker will certainly be the larger of the two types. Consider the storage or bench space when you're choosing which size, shape and type to buy. We used a 6-litre (24-cup) pressure cooker for the recipes in this book.

STOVE-TOP PRESSURE COOKERS

Stove-top cookers made from aluminium or stainless steel are suitable for either gas or electric cook tops – you will need to buy stainless steel though if you have a ceramic or an induction stove-top. Price is a good guide to quality. The size and shape you choose will depend on your family's needs. Do your research and look at the cookers carefully; lift them to see if you can manage the weight and like the feel of the handle/s. Position the lids a few times to make sure you're comfortable handling them. When it's time to release the pressure of the cooker, do this off the heat.

BENCH-TOP PRESSURE COOKERS

These cookers, once set, just get on with the job of reaching the required pressure then stabilising, before the cook steps in to release the pressure and remove the lid.

THE QUICK RELEASE METHOD

For the quick release method referred to in our recipes use tongs (steam can burn your fingers) to turn the pressure valve on top of the cooker to open the valve and release the steam. This will release the pressure quickly, before you remove the lid. If you need to check the food towards the end of the suggested cooking time or add more ingredients to the cooker, follow the quick release method.

DO

• read your instruction manual thoroughly before you use the pressure cooker
• read cooking times carefully; start timing the food after the pressure is reached
• fill the cooker up to the marked line inside the cooker – no more
• release the lid carefully, in an open space, facing away from you to avoid the escaping steam
• use a trivet – usually provided – for steaming puddings etc
• time your pressure cooking carefully – follow the recipes
• wash and dry the cooker and removable gasket well after use
• use a simmer mat to keep the heat as low as possible after a cooker has reached pressure
• use tongs – not your fingers – to release the pressure from the cooker
• wash the bases of pressure cookers in the dishwasher, after checking the manual
• store the pressure cooker with its lid on upside-down

DON'T

• leave the cooker on and unattended
• over-fill the cooker with food or liquid
• cook pasta or porridge, or any food that becomes foamy in a pressure cooker
• soak the bases of pressure cookers
• wash the lid of a cooker in a dishwasher – it will damage the valve

SPICY CHICKPEA AND LENTIL SOUP

prep + cook time 40 minutes (+ standing)
makes 2.5 litres (10 cups)
nutritional count per 1 cup 2.4g total fat (0.4g saturated
fat); 568kJ (136 cal); 17.2g carbohydrate; 8.5g protein;
6.1g fibre

1 cup (200g) dried chickpeas (garbanzo beans)
2 teaspoons olive oil
1 medium brown onion (150g), chopped finely
3 cloves garlic, crushed
4cm (1½-inch) piece fresh ginger (20g), grated
2 teaspoons smoked paprika
1 teaspoon each ground coriander and cumin
½ teaspoon dried chilli flakes
410g (13 ounces) canned crushed tomatoes
3 cups (750ml) water
3 cups (750ml) chicken stock
2 stalks celery (300g), trimmed, sliced thickly
470g (15 ounces) pumpkin, cut into
    1cm (½-inch) pieces
1 cup (200g) red lentils, rinsed, drained
2 tablespoons lime juice
½ cup coarsely chopped fresh coriander
    (cilantro)

1 Place chickpeas in medium bowl, cover with
cold water; stand overnight. Rinse under cold
water; drain.
2 Heat oil in 6-litre (24-cup) pressure cooker;
cook onion, garlic and ginger, stirring, until onion
softens. Add spices; cook, stirring, until fragrant.
Add undrained tomatoes, the water, stock and
chickpeas; secure lid. Bring cooker to high
pressure. Reduce heat to stabilise pressure;
cook 25 minutes.
3 Release pressure using the quick release
method (page 5); remove lid. Add celery,
pumpkin and lentils; secure lid. Bring cooker
to high pressure. Reduce heat to stabilise
pressure; cook 5 minutes.
4 Release pressure using the quick release
method (page 5); remove lid. Stir in juice and
coriander; season to taste.

tips If you have an electric pressure cooker you won't
need to reduce the heat to stabilise pressure, your cooker
will automatically stabilise itself. Always check with the
manufacturer's instructions before using. Recipe suitable
to freeze.

SOUP

CHICKEN AND RICE SOUP

prep + cook time **30 minutes** makes **2.75 litres (11 cups)**
nutritional count per 1 cup **11.4g total fat (2.9g
saturated fat); 698kJ (167 cal); 6.9g carbohydrate;
8.7g protein; 1.5g fibre**

2 teaspoons olive oil
1 large brown onion (200g), chopped finely
⅓ cup (65g) white long-grain rice
1 large tomato (220g), chopped finely
1 tablespoon drained, finely chopped,
   pickled jalapeño chillies
1 cup coarsely chopped fresh coriander
   (cilantro)
1 large avocado (320g), chopped finely
chicken stock
½ chicken (800g)
1 medium carrot (120g), halved
1 small brown onion (80g), halved
1 stalk celery (150g), halved
1 teaspoon black peppercorns
1.5 litres (6 cups) water

1 Make chicken stock. Discard skin and bones
from chicken; shred meat coarsely.
2 Heat oil in 6-litre (24-cup) pressure cooker;
cook onion, stirring, until soft. Add rice; stir to
coat in onion mixture. Add stock; secure lid.
Bring cooker to high pressure. Reduce heat
to stabilise pressure; cook 5 minutes.
3 Release pressure using the quick release
method (page 5); remove lid. Return chicken
to cooker with tomato and chilli; simmer,
uncovered, until hot. Stir in coriander; season
to taste. Serve soup topped with avocado.
chicken stock Combine ingredients in 6-litre
(24-cup) pressure cooker; secure lid. Bring
cooker to high pressure. Reduce heat to
stabilise pressure; cook 15 minutes. Release
pressure using the quick release method (page
5); remove lid. Strain stock into large heatproof
bowl. Reserve chicken; discard vegetables
and pepper.

tips If you have an electric pressure cooker you won't
need to reduce the heat to stabilise pressure, your
cooker will automatically stabilise itself. Always check
with the manufacturer's instructions before using.
If making chicken stock for another recipe where
you only need the stock, use chicken necks, wings
and backs instead of the half chicken. The stock will
keep refrigerated for up to 1 week, or frozen for up
to 2 months.

SCOTCH BROTH

prep + cook time 40 minutes makes 3 litres (12 cups)
nutritional count per 1 cup 9.5g total fat (3.7g
saturated fat); 727kJ (174 cal); 7.4g carbohydrate;
13.6g protein; 2.8g fibre

1 tablespoon olive oil
1kg (2 pounds) lamb neck chops
½ cup (100g) pearl barley
1 large brown onion (200g),
    chopped coarsely
2 stalks celery (300g), trimmed,
    chopped coarsely
1 large carrot (180g), sliced thickly
1.5 litres (6 cups) water
3 cups (240g) finely shredded
    savoy cabbage
¾ cup coarsely chopped fresh
    flat-leaf parsley

1 Heat oil in 6-litre (24-cup) pressure cooker;
cook lamb, in batches, until browned. Remove
from cooker.
2 Return lamb to cooker with barley, onion,
celery, carrot and the water; secure lid.
Bring cooker to high pressure. Reduce heat
to stabilise pressure; cook 20 minutes.
3 Release pressure using the quick release
method (page 5); remove lid. Remove lamb
with slotted spoon. Add cabbage to cooker;
secure lid. Bring cooker to high pressure. Reduce
heat to stabilise pressure; cook 5 minutes.
4 Meanwhile, remove meat from lamb chops;
discard bones, chop meat coarsely.
5 Release pressure using the quick release
method (page 5); remove lid. Stir in lamb and
parsley; season to taste.

tips If you have an electric pressure cooker you won't
need to reduce the heat to stabilise pressure, your
cooker will automatically stabilise itself. Always check
with the manufacturer's instructions before using.
Recipe suitable to freeze.

HARIRA

prep + cook time 1 hour 10 minutes (+ standing)
makes 3 litres (12 cups)
nutritional count per 1 cup 5.6g total fat (1.2g
saturated fat); 606kJ (145 cal); 11.3g carbohydrate;
10.4g protein; 4.3g fibre

1 cup (200g) dried chickpeas (garbanzo
  beans)
2.5 litres (10 cups) water
2 tablespoons olive oil
2 french-trimmed lamb shanks (500g)
1 large brown onion (200g), chopped finely
3 cloves garlic, crushed
1 teaspoon ground cinnamon
½ teaspoon each ground turmeric and ginger
410g (13 ounces) canned diced tomatoes
½ cup (100g) brown lentils, rinsed, drained
¼ cup (60ml) lemon juice
1 cup coarsely chopped fresh coriander
  (cilantro)

1 Place chickpeas in medium bowl, cover with
cold water; stand overnight. Rinse under cold
water; drain.
2 Combine chickpeas and 3 cups (750ml) of
the water in 6-litre (24-cup) pressure cooker;
secure lid. Bring cooker to high pressure.
Reduce heat to stabilise pressure; cook
10 minutes. Release pressure using the
quick release method (page 5); remove lid.
Drain chickpeas.

3 Heat oil in cooker; cook lamb until browned.
Remove from cooker.
4 Cook onion and garlic in cooker, stirring, until
onion softens. Add spices; cook, stirring, until
fragrant. Return lamb to cooker with undrained
tomatoes and the remaining water; secure lid.
Bring cooker to high pressure. Reduce heat to
stabilise pressure; cook 25 minutes.
5 Release pressure using the quick release
method (page 5); remove lid. Add lentils and
chickpeas; secure lid. Bring cooker to high
pressure. Reduce heat to stabilise pressure;
cook 15 minutes. Release pressure using the
quick release method (page 5); remove lid.
Remove lamb with slotted spoon.
6 When lamb is cool enough to handle, shred
meat coarsely, discard bones. Return lamb to
cooker with juice; simmer, uncovered, until hot.
Season to taste. Serve soup topped with
coriander.

tips If you have an electric pressure cooker you won't
need to reduce the heat to stabilise pressure, your
cooker will automatically stabilise itself. Always check
with the manufacturer's instructions before using.
If you forget to, or can't soak the chickpeas overnight,
simply cook them for 35 minutes instead of 10 in 6 cups
of water instead of 3. You need to cook the chickpeas
separately as they don't become tender if cooked with
acid (tomatoes) or salt. Harira is a traditional Moroccan
soup often served at night during Ramadan to break the
fasting day. This recipe is suitable to freeze.

CLASSIC MINESTRONE

prep + cook time 35 minutes makes 3.5 litres (14 cups)
nutritional count per 1 cup 3.4g total fat (1.4g saturated
fat); 581kJ (139 cal); 11.4g carbohydrate; 14.2g protein;
3.6g fibre

1 ham hock (1kg)
1 medium brown onion (150g)
1 stalk celery (150g), trimmed, halved
1 teaspoon black peppercorns
1 dried bay leaf
1.5 litres (6 cups) water
2 cups (360g) cooked white beans
1 large carrot (180g), chopped coarsely
2 medium zucchini (240g), chopped coarsely
2 stalks celery (300g), extra, trimmed,
    chopped coarsely
3 cloves garlic, crushed
410g (13 ounces) canned diced tomatoes
1 cup (100g) small pasta shells
1 cup coarsely chopped fresh basil leaves
½ cup (40g) grated parmesan cheese

1 Combine ham, onion, halved celery, peppercorns, bay leaf and the water in 6-litre (24-cup) pressure cooker; secure lid. Bring cooker to high pressure. Reduce heat to stabilise pressure; cook 20 minutes.
2 Release pressure using the quick release method (page 5); remove lid. Strain stock into large heatproof bowl; reserve ham, discard vegetables and peppercorns. When ham is cool enough to handle, remove meat from bone; discard bone, skin and fat, shred ham coarsely.
3 Return stock to cooker with shredded ham, beans, carrot, zucchini, chopped celery, garlic, undrained tomatoes and pasta; secure lid. Bring cooker to high pressure. Reduce heat to stabilise pressure; cook 3 minutes.
4 Release pressure using the quick release method (page 5); remove lid. Season to taste. Serve soup sprinkled with basil and cheese.

tips If you have an electric pressure cooker you won't need to reduce the heat to stabilise pressure, your cooker will automatically stabilise itself. Always check with the manufacturer's instructions before using. You'll need to cook 1 cup (200g) of dried white beans for this recipe. If soaked overnight, they take 10 minutes to cook in a pressure cooker. You can use any white bean you like. Recipe not suitable to freeze.

LAMB SHANK, VEGETABLE AND LENTIL SOUP

prep + cook time 40 minutes makes 2 litres (8 cups)
nutritional count per 1 cup 10.5g total fat (3g saturated
fat); 957kJ (229 cal); 9.5g carbohydrate; 19.6g protein;
4.2g fibre

2 tablespoons olive oil
3 french-trimmed lamb shanks (750g)
1 medium brown onion (150g),
    chopped finely
2 cloves garlic, crushed
2 medium carrots (240g), chopped coarsely
2 stalks celery (300g), trimmed,
    chopped coarsely
155g (5-ounce) piece pancetta,
    chopped coarsely
1.25 litres (5 cups) water
½ cup (125ml) dry white wine
⅔ cup (130g) french-style green lentils,
    rinsed, drained
½ cup (60g) frozen peas

1 Heat half the oil in 6-litre (24-cup) pressure cooker; cook lamb, in batches, until browned. Remove from cooker.
2 Heat remaining oil in cooker; cook onion, garlic, carrot, celery and pancetta, stirring, until vegetables soften. Return lamb to cooker with the water and wine; secure lid. Bring cooker to high pressure. Reduce heat to stabilise pressure; cook 20 minutes.
3 Release pressure using the quick release method (page 5); remove lid. Add lentils; secure lid. Bring cooker to high pressure. Reduce heat to stabilise pressure; cook 10 minutes.
4 Release pressure using the quick release method (page 5); remove lid. Remove lamb; when cool enough to handle shred meat coarsely, discard bones. Return lamb to cooker with peas; simmer, uncovered until peas are tender. Season to taste.

tips If you have an electric pressure cooker you won't need to reduce the heat to stabilise pressure, your cooker will automatically stabilise itself. Always check with the manufacturer's instructions before using. Recipe suitable to freeze.

PEA, HAM AND BROAD BEAN SOUP

prep + cook time **1 hour 10 minutes**
makes **1.5 litres (6 cups)**
nutritional count per 1 cup **18.3g total fat (3.5g
saturated fat); 1751kJ (419 cal); 32g carbohydrate;
26.1g protein; 11.1g fibre**

1 tablespoon olive oil
1 large brown onion (200g), chopped coarsely
2 cloves garlic, crushed
2 stalks celery (300g), trimmed,
   chopped coarsely
1 medium carrot (120g), chopped coarsely
1 ham hock (750g)
2 dried bay leaves
2 litres (8 cups) water
1½ cups (225g) frozen broad beans
   (fava beans), thawed, peeled
1½ cups (300g) green split peas,
   rinsed, drained
mint sauce
2 cups loosely packed fresh mint leaves
¼ cup (60ml) olive oil
2 tablespoons white wine vinegar
2 teaspoons caster (superfine) sugar

1 Heat oil in 6-litre (24-cup) pressure cooker;
cook onion, garlic, celery and carrot, stirring,
about 3 minutes or until vegetables soften.
Add ham, bay leaves and the water; secure lid.
Bring cooker to high pressure. Reduce heat to
stabilise pressure; cook 20 minutes.
2 Release pressure using the quick release
method (page 5); remove lid. Add beans
and peas; secure lid. Bring cooker to high
pressure. Reduce heat to stabilise pressure;
cook 20 minutes.
3 Release pressure using the quick release
method (page 5); remove lid. Discard bay
leaves. Remove ham. Cool soup 10 minutes.
4 Meanwhile, discard skin, fat and bone from
ham; shred meat coarsely.
5 Blend or process soup, in batches, until
smooth. Return soup to cooker; stir in ham.
Simmer, uncovered, until hot; season to taste.
6 Meanwhile, make mint sauce.
7 Serve bowls of soup drizzled with mint sauce.
mint sauce Blend ingredients until smooth.

tips **If you have an electric pressure cooker you won't
need to reduce the heat to stabilise pressure, your
cooker will automatically stabilise itself. Always check
with the manufacturer's instructions before using. Soup
suitable to freeze; mint sauce not suitable to freeze.**

COQ AU VIN

prep + cook time 30 minutes serves 4
nutritional count per serving 47.7g total fat (13.9g
saturated fat); 3035kJ (726 cal); 10g carbohydrate;
53.5g protein; 2.2g fibre

12 baby brown onions (300g)
2 tablespoons olive oil
3 rindless bacon slices (195g),
   chopped coarsely
315g (10 ounces) button mushrooms
3 cloves garlic, crushed
2 tablespoons plain (all-purpose) flour
4 chicken thigh cutlets (800g)
4 chicken drumsticks (600g)
¼ cup (70g) tomato paste
1 cup (250ml) dry red wine
2 dried bay leaves
6 sprigs fresh thyme

1 Peel onions, leaving root ends intact.
Heat 2 teaspoons of the oil in 6-litre (24-cup)
pressure cooker; cook onions, stirring, until
browned lightly. Remove from cooker.
2 Heat another 2 teaspoons of the oil in
cooker; cook bacon, mushrooms and garlic,
stirring, until browned lightly. Remove from
cooker.
3 Season flour in large bowl; add chicken,
toss to coat in flour. Shake off excess. Heat
remaining oil in cooker; cook chicken, in
batches, until browned. Remove from cooker.
4 Return chicken to cooker with onions,
bacon mixture, paste, wine, bay leaves and
thyme; secure lid. Bring cooker to high
pressure. Reduce heat to stabilise pressure;
cook 10 minutes.
5 Release pressure using the quick release
method (page 5); remove lid. Season to taste;
serve sprinkled with extra thyme leaves.

tips If you have an electric pressure cooker you won't
need to reduce the heat to stabilise pressure, your
cooker will automatically stabilise itself. Always check
with the manufacturer's instructions before using.
Recipe not suitable to freeze.
serving suggestion Serve with mashed potato.

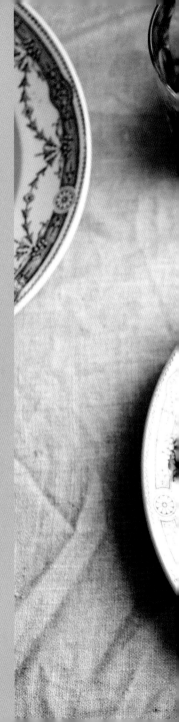

CHICKEN

BUTTER CHICKEN

prep + cook time 40 minutes serves 4
nutritional count per serving 58.1g total fat (23.5g
saturated fat); 3403kJ (814 cal); 23.5g carbohydrate;
48.7g protein; 4g fibre

4 chicken marylands (1.4kg)
1 tablespoon lemon juice
½ cup (140g) yogurt
5cm (2-inch) piece fresh ginger (25g), grated
2 teaspoons garam masala
1 tablespoon vegetable oil
40g (1½ ounces) butter
1 medium brown onion (150g),
   chopped finely
4 cloves garlic, crushed
1 teaspoon each ground coriander, cumin,
   cinnamon and hot paprika
2 tablespoons tomato paste
410g (13 ounces) canned tomato puree
½ cup (125ml) chicken stock
2 tablespoons honey
⅓ cup (80ml) pouring cream
½ cup loosely packed fresh coriander
   (cilantro) leaves

1 Combine chicken, juice, yogurt, ginger and
garam masala in large bowl. Heat half the oil
and half the butter in 6-litre (24-cup) pressure
cooker; cook chicken, in batches, until
browned. Remove from cooker.
2 Heat remaining oil and butter in cooker;
cook onion and garlic, stirring, until onion
softens. Add spices; cook, stirring, until
fragrant. Return chicken to cooker with paste,
puree, stock and honey; secure lid. Bring
cooker to high pressure. Reduce heat to
stabilise pressure; cook 20 minutes.
3 Release pressure using the quick release
method (page 5); remove lid. Stir in cream;
season to taste. Serve chicken sprinkled
with coriander.

tips If you have an electric pressure cooker you won't
need to reduce the heat to stabilise pressure, your
cooker will automatically stabilise itself. Always check
with the manufacturer's instructions before using.
Recipe not suitable to freeze.
serving suggestion Serve with steamed basmati rice.

CHICKEN CACCIATORE

prep + cook time 30 minutes serves 4
nutritional count per serving 41.6g total fat (11.6g
saturated fat); 2587kJ (619 cal); 10.6g carbohydrate;
44.6g protein; 3.2g fibre

2 tablespoons olive oil
4 chicken thigh cutlets (800g)
4 chicken drumsticks (600g)
1 medium brown onion (150g), sliced thinly
2 cloves garlic, crushed
2 drained anchovy fillets, chopped finely
2 tablespoons white wine vinegar
¼ cup (70g) tomato paste
½ cup (125ml) dry red wine
410g (13 ounces) canned crushed tomatoes
½ cup (60g) seeded black olives
½ cup coarsely chopped fresh
   flat-leaf parsley

1 Heat half the oil in 6-litre (24-cup) pressure cooker; cook chicken, in batches, until browned. Remove from cooker.
2 Heat remaining oil in cooker; cook onion, garlic and anchovy, stirring, until onion softens. Return chicken to cooker with vinegar, paste, wine and undrained tomatoes; secure lid. Bring cooker to high pressure. Reduce heat to stabilise pressure; cook 10 minutes.
3 Release pressure using the quick release method (page 5); remove lid. Stir in olives; season to taste. Serve chicken sprinkled with parsley.

tips If you have an electric pressure cooker you won't need to reduce the heat to stabilise pressure, your cooker will automatically stabilise itself. Always check with the manufacturer's instructions before using. Recipe suitable to freeze.
serving suggestion Serve with creamy mashed potato or crusty bread.

GREEN CHICKEN CURRY

prep + cook time **20 minutes** serves **4**
nutritional count per serving 41.6g total fat (18.3g
saturated fat); 2562kJ (613 cal); 8.6g carbohydrate;
50.1g protein; 4.4g fibre

1 tablespoon peanut oil
1kg (2 pounds) chicken thigh fillets,
    quartered
¼ cup (75g) green curry paste
1 cup (250ml) coconut cream
2 medium zucchini (240g), sliced thickly
1 tablespoon fish sauce
1 tablespoon lime juice
1 tablespoon grated palm sugar
⅓ cup each loosely packed fresh coriander
    (cilantro) and thai basil leaves
2 green onions (scallions), sliced thinly

1 Heat half the oil in 6-litre (24-cup) pressure
cooker; cook chicken, in batches, until
browned. Remove from cooker.
2 Heat remaining oil in cooker; cook paste,
stirring, about 3 minutes or until fragrant. Return
chicken to cooker with coconut cream; secure
lid. Bring cooker to high pressure. Reduce
heat to stabilise pressure; cook 5 minutes.
3 Release pressure using the quick release
method (page 5); remove lid. Add zucchini;
secure lid. Bring cooker to high pressure. Reduce
heat to stabilise pressure; cook 2 minutes.
4 Release pressure using the quick release
method (page 5); remove lid. Stir in sauce,
juice, sugar and half the herbs; season to taste.
Serve curry sprinkled with remaining herbs
and onion.

tips If you have an electric pressure cooker you won't
need to reduce the heat to stabilise pressure, your
cooker will automatically stabilise itself. Always check
with the manufacturer's instructions before using.
Recipe not suitable to freeze.
serving suggestion Serve with steamed jasmine rice.

CHICKEN AND FIG TAGINE

prep + cook time 30 minutes serves 4
nutritional count per serving 39g total fat (8.5g saturated fat); 2742kJ (656 cal); 25.9g carbohydrate; 48g protein; 7.5g fibre

2 tablespoons plain (all-purpose) flour
4 single chicken breasts on the bone (1kg)
2 tablespoons olive oil
1 large red onion (300g), sliced thinly
2 cloves garlic, crushed
2 teaspoons each ground coriander, cumin, ginger and cinnamon
pinch saffron threads
¾ cup (180ml) chicken stock
1 tablespoon honey
315g (10 ounces) spinach, trimmed, shredded coarsely
6 medium fresh figs (360g), halved
1 teaspoon caster (superfine) sugar
2 tablespoons each coarsely chopped fresh flat-leaf parsley and coriander (cilantro)
½ cup (70g) coarsely chopped, roasted unsalted pistachios

1 Season flour in large bowl; add chicken, toss to coat in flour. Shake off excess. Heat half the oil in 6-litre (24-cup) pressure cooker; cook chicken, in batches, until browned. Remove from cooker.
2 Heat remaining oil in cooker; cook onion, garlic and spices, stirring, until onion softens. Return chicken to cooker with stock and honey; secure lid. Bring cooker to high pressure. Reduce heat to stabilise pressure; cook 15 minutes.
3 Release pressure using the quick release method (page 5); remove lid. Remove chicken; cover to keep warm. Stir spinach into cooker; season to taste.
4 Place figs, cut-side up, on oven tray; sprinkle with sugar. Cook under preheated grill (broiler) about 5 minutes or until browned lightly.
5 Return chicken to cooker; simmer, uncovered, until hot. Serve tagine with figs; sprinkle with herbs and nuts.

tips If you have an electric pressure cooker you won't need to reduce the heat to stabilise pressure, your cooker will automatically stabilise itself. Always check with the manufacturer's instructions before using. Recipe suitable to freeze without figs.

CHICKEN WITH CAPSICUM

prep + cook time **30 minutes** serves **4**

nutritional count per serving 25g total fat (7.3g saturated fat); 1634kJ (391 cal); 10.1g carbohydrate; 27g protein; 3g fibre

1 tablespoon olive oil
4 chicken thigh cutlets (800g)
2 medium brown onions (300g), sliced thinly
3 cloves garlic, crushed
2 medium red capsicums (bell peppers) (400g), sliced thickly
2 medium yellow capsicums (bell peppers) (400g), sliced thickly
1 tablespoon tomato paste
⅓ cup (80ml) dry white wine
⅓ cup (80ml) chicken stock
2 dried bay leaves
4 sprigs fresh thyme
2 teaspoons finely chopped fresh thyme

1 Heat half the oil in 6-litre (24-cup) pressure cooker; cook chicken, in batches, until browned. Remove from cooker.
2 Heat remaining oil in cooker; cook onion, garlic and capsicum, stirring, until onion softens. Add paste; cook, stirring, 1 minute. Return chicken to cooker with wine, stock, bay leaves and thyme sprigs; secure lid. Bring cooker to high pressure. Reduce heat to stabilise pressure; cook 15 minutes.
3 Release pressure using the quick release method (page 5); remove lid. Season to taste. Serve sprinkled with chopped thyme.

tips If you have an electric pressure cooker you won't need to reduce the heat to stabilise pressure, your cooker will automatically stabilise itself. Always check with the manufacturer's instructions before using. Recipe suitable to freeze.
serving suggestion Serve with mashed potatoes.

BEEF BOURGUIGNON

prep + cook time 1 hour serves 6
nutritional count per serving 25.9g total fat (8g
saturated fat); 1935kJ (463 cal); 6.1g carbohydrate;
45.7g protein; 3.3g fibre

1½ tablespoons olive oil
400g (12½ ounces) button mushrooms
1 dried bay leaf
3 sprigs fresh parsley
1 sprig fresh thyme
1kg (2 pounds) gravy beef, chopped coarsely
150g (4½ ounces) speck, chopped coarsely
1 medium brown onion (150g),
    chopped finely
3 cloves garlic, crushed
⅔ cup (160ml) dry red wine
¼ cup (70g) tomato paste
12 baby onions (300g)

1 Heat 2 teaspoons of the oil in 6-litre (24-cup)
pressure cooker; cook mushrooms until
browned. Remove from cooker.
2 Tie bay leaf, parsley and thyme together
with kitchen string to make a bouquet garni.
Heat remaining oil in cooker; cook beef, in
batches, until browned. Remove from cooker.
3 Cook speck in cooker until browned.
Add chopped onion and garlic; cook, stirring,
until onion softens. Return beef to cooker
with wine, paste and bouquet garni; secure lid.
Bring cooker to high pressure. Reduce heat
to stabilise pressure; cook 35 minutes.
4 Meanwhile, peel baby onions, leaving root
ends intact.
5 Release pressure using the quick release
method (page 5); remove lid. Add baby onions
and mushrooms; secure lid. Bring cooker
to high pressure. Reduce heat to stabilise
pressure; cook 10 minutes. Release pressure
using the quick release method (page 5);
remove lid. Discard bouquet garni. Season
to taste.

tips If you have an electric pressure cooker you won't
need to reduce the heat to stabilise pressure, your
cooker will automatically stabilise itself. Always check
with the manufacturer's instructions before using.
Recipe not suitable to freeze.
serving suggestion Serve with mashed potatoes.

BEEF
& VEAL

CHILLI CON CARNE

prep + cook time **40 minutes (+ standing)** serves **6**
nutritional count per serving **34.9g total fat (15.3g
saturated fat); 2913kJ (697 cal); 36.1g carbohydrate;
51.3g protein; 17.1g fibre**

2 cups (400g) dried red kidney beans
3 small brown onions (240g)
1 dried bay leaf
1.5 litres (6 cups) water
150g (4½ ounces) speck, chopped finely
1 cured chorizo sausage (170g),
    chopped finely
400g (12½ ounces) minced (ground) beef
2 cloves garlic, crushed
2 tablespoons ground cumin
1 tablespoon ground coriander
1 teaspoon dried chilli flakes
2 cups (560g) bottled tomato pasta sauce
2 teaspoons dried oregano
½ cup (120g) sour cream
½ cup loosely packed fresh coriander
    (cilantro) leaves

1 Place beans in large bowl, cover with cold water; stand overnight. Rinse under cold water; drain.
2 Combine beans, one of the onions, bay leaf and the water in 6-litre (24-cup) pressure cooker; secure lid. Bring cooker to high pressure. Reduce heat to stabilise pressure; cook 15 minutes. Release pressure using the quick release method (page 5); remove lid. Drain beans, reserving 1½ cups (375ml) cooking liquid; discard onion and bay leaf.
3 Finely chop remaining onions. Cook speck and chorizo in cooker until browned. Add onion; cook, stirring, until onion softens. Add beef; cook, stirring, until browned. Add garlic and spices; cook, stirring, until fragrant. Return beans to cooker with sauce, oregano and reserved cooking liquid; season to taste. Bring cooker to high pressure. Reduce heat to stabilise pressure; cook 8 minutes. Release pressure using the quick release method (page 5); remove lid. Stand 5 minutes.
4 Serve chilli con carne with sour cream and sprinkle with coriander.

tips If you have an electric pressure cooker you won't need to reduce the heat to stabilise pressure, your cooker will automatically stabilise itself. Always check with the manufacturer's instructions before using. If you normally eat chilli con carne with sour cream but are trying to be good, try it with a dollop of light Greek-style yogurt instead. Recipe suitable to freeze.

BEEF CHEEKS WITH RED WINE

prep + cook time **50 minutes** serves **6**
nutritional count per serving **19.5g total fat (6.5g
saturated fat); 1626kJ (389 cal); 11.3g carbohydrate;
36.9g protein; 3.7g fibre**

12 baby brown onions (300g)
2 tablespoons olive oil
2 tablespoons plain (all-purpose) flour
1kg (2 pounds) beef cheeks,
   chopped coarsely
1 dried bay leaf
3 sprigs fresh parsley
1 sprig fresh thyme
1 large brown onion (200g), chopped finely
3 cloves garlic, crushed
½ cup (125ml) dry red wine
¼ cup (60ml) water
3 large carrots (540g), chopped coarsely
1½ tablespoons balsamic vinegar glaze

1 Peel baby onions, leaving root ends intact.
Heat 2 teaspoons of the oil in 6-litre (24-cup)
pressure cooker; cook baby onions, stirring,
about 5 minutes or until browned lightly all over.
Remove from cooker.
2 Season flour in large bowl; add beef, toss to
coat in flour. Shake off excess. Heat half the oil
in cooker; cook beef, in batches, until browned.
Remove from cooker.

3 Tie bay leaf, parsley and thyme together
with kitchen string to make a bouquet garni.
Heat remaining oil in cooker; cook chopped
onion and garlic, stirring, until onion softens.
Return beef to cooker with wine, the water and
bouquet garni; secure lid. Bring cooker to high
pressure. Reduce heat to stabilise pressure;
cook 20 minutes.
4 Release pressure using the quick release
method (page 5); remove lid. Add baby onions
and carrots; secure lid. Bring cooker to high
pressure. Reduce heat to stabilise pressure;
cook 5 minutes. Release pressure using the
quick release method (page 5); remove lid.
Stir in glaze; season to taste. Serve sprinkled
with chopped parsley, if you like.

tips If you have an electric pressure cooker you won't
need to reduce the heat to stabilise pressure, your
cooker will automatically stabilise itself. Always check
with the manufacturer's instructions before using.
You can use chuck or gravy beef for this recipe, but
beef cheek is an amazing cut of meat; cooked long
enough (or in a pressure cooker) it melts in your mouth.
Recipe suitable to freeze.
serving suggestion Serve with mashed potatoes and
your favourite steamed green vegetables.

BEEF TAGINE WITH SPINACH AND OLIVES

prep + cook time 30 minutes serves 4
nutritional count per serving 30.5g total fat (9.8g saturated fat); 2537kJ (607 cal); 11.3g carbohydrate; 69g protein; 5.4g fibre

1 tablespoon olive oil
1.2kg (2½ pounds) beef blade steak, trimmed, chopped coarsely
1 medium brown onion (150g), chopped finely
2 cloves garlic, crushed
1 teaspoon each ground allspice and dried chilli flakes
pinch saffron threads
410g (13 ounces) canned crushed tomatoes
½ cup (125ml) beef stock
300g (9½ ounces) spinach, trimmed, shredded coarsely
½ cup (60g) seeded green olives
2 tablespoons thinly sliced preserved lemon rind
⅓ cup (45g) coarsely chopped, roasted unsalted pistachios

1 Heat half the oil in 6-litre (24-cup) pressure cooker; cook beef, in batches, until browned. Remove from cooker.
2 Heat remaining oil in cooker; cook onion, garlic and spices, stirring, until onion softens. Return beef to cooker with undrained tomatoes and stock; secure lid. Bring cooker to high pressure. Reduce heat to stabilise pressure; cook 15 minutes.
3 Release pressure using the quick release method (page 5); remove lid. Stir in spinach, olives and preserved lemon; simmer, uncovered, until hot. Season to taste. Serve tagine sprinkled with nuts.

tips If you have an electric pressure cooker you won't need to reduce the heat to stabilise pressure, your cooker will automatically stabilise itself. Always check with the manufacturer's instructions before using. Preserved lemons, a prominent ingredient in North African cooking, are salted lemons bottled for several months; the flavour is salty, unique and perfumed. To use, discard flesh, rinse well, using the rind only. Recipe not suitable to freeze.
serving suggestion Serve with couscous.

VEAL MARSALA AND MUSHROOMS

prep + cook time **25 minutes** serves **4**
nutritional count per serving 27.1g total fat (13.8g
saturated fat); 2433kJ (582 cal); 11.2g carbohydrate;
66.1g protein; 3.3g fibre

2 tablespoons plain (all-purpose) flour
1kg (2 pounds) diced veal
1 tablespoon olive oil
20g (¾ ounce) butter
1 medium brown onion (150g),
    chopped finely
2 cloves garlic, crushed
⅓ cup (80ml) marsala
½ cup (125ml) beef stock
375g (12 ounces) mixed mushrooms,
    sliced thickly
½ cup (125ml) pouring cream
2 teaspoons finely chopped lemon thyme

1 Season flour in large bowl; add veal, toss to
coat in flour. Shake off excess. Heat half the oil
and half the butter in 6-litre (24-cup) pressure
cooker; cook veal, in batches, until browned.
Remove the veal from cooker.
2 Heat remaining oil and butter in cooker; cook
onion and garlic, stirring, until onion softens.
Add marsala; simmer, uncovered, until liquid
reduces by half. Return veal to cooker with
stock; secure lid. Bring cooker to high
pressure. Reduce heat to stabilise pressure;
cook 10 minutes.
3 Release pressure using the quick release
method (page 5); remove lid. Add mushrooms;
secure lid. Bring cooker to high pressure. Reduce
heat to stabilise pressure; cook 3 minutes.
4 Release pressure using the quick release
method (page 5); remove lid. Stir in cream;
simmer, uncovered, until sauce thickens
slightly. Season to taste. Serve veal sprinkled
with thyme.

tips If you have an electric pressure cooker you won't
need to reduce the heat to stabilise pressure, your
cooker will automatically stabilise itself. Always check
with the manufacturer's instructions before using.
Ask the butcher for any stewing veal, such as shoulder.
Recipe not suitable to freeze.
serving suggestion Serve with your favourite pasta or
creamy mashed potato.

OSSO BUCO WITH OLIVES, BASIL AND ANCHOVIES

prep + cook time **40 minutes** serves **6**

nutritional count per serving 6.3g total fat (1.3g
saturated fat); 1154kJ (276 cal); 6.3g carbohydrate;
43.8g protein; 1.7g fibre

1 tablespoon olive oil
6 thick pieces veal osso buco (1.8kg)
1 large brown onion (200g), chopped finely
2 cloves garlic, crushed
6 drained anchovy fillets, chopped finely
¼ cup coarsely chopped fresh basil
410g (13 ounces) canned crushed tomatoes
½ cup (125ml) dry red wine
½ cup (80g) coarsely chopped seeded
   black olives
⅓ cup loosely packed fresh small
   basil leaves

1 Heat oil in 6-litre (24-cup) pressure cooker;
cook veal, in batches, until browned. Remove
from cooker.
2 Cook onion, garlic, anchovy and chopped
basil in cooker, stirring, until onion softens.
Return veal to cooker with undrained tomatoes
and wine; secure lid. Bring cooker to high
pressure. Reduce heat to stabilise pressure;
cook 30 minutes.
3 Release pressure using the quick release
method (page 5); remove lid. Stir in olives;
season to taste.
4 Serve veal with sauce; top with basil leaves.

tips If you have an electric pressure cooker you won't
need to reduce the heat to stabilise pressure, your
cooker will automatically stabilise itself. Always check
with the manufacturer's instructions before using.
Recipe suitable to freeze.
serving suggestion Serve with creamy polenta or
mashed potatoes.

CORNED BEEF

prep + cook time 1 hour (+ standing) serves 6
nutritional count per serving 7.1g total fat (3g saturated fat); 1116kJ (267 cal); 6.7g carbohydrate; 43.1g protein; 1.1g fibre

1.5kg (3-pound) piece corned beef silverside
1 medium brown onion (150g),
    chopped coarsely
2 dried bay leaves
6 black peppercorns
1 medium carrot (120g), chopped coarsely
1 stalk celery (150g), trimmed,
    chopped coarsely
2 tablespoons light brown sugar
2 tablespoons malt vinegar
1.5 litres (6 cups) water, approximately

1 Combine beef, onion, bay leaves, peppercorns, carrot, celery, sugar, vinegar and enough of the water to barely cover beef in 6-litre (24-cup) pressure cooker; secure lid. Bring cooker to high pressure. Reduce heat to stabilise pressure; cook 45 minutes.
2 Release pressure using the quick release method (page 5); remove lid. Stand beef in cooking liquid 15 minutes. Remove beef from cooker. Serve sliced, warm or cold.

tips If you have an electric pressure cooker you won't need to reduce the heat to stabilise pressure, your cooker will automatically stabilise itself. Always check with the manufacturer's instructions before using. If corned beef is to be served cold, cool the beef in the cooking liquid before refrigerating. Recipe not suitable to freeze.
serving suggestion Serve warm corned beef with creamy mashed potato, mustard, cornichons, caperberries and parsley or with steamed potatoes, carrots and cabbage. Serve thin slices of cold corned beef in sandwiches with pickles.

LAMB NAVARIN

prep + cook time 40 minutes serves 4
nutritional count per serving 21.9g total fat (8.3g
saturated fat); 1994kJ (477 cal); 31.2g carbohydrate;
34g protein; 9.6g fibre

1 tablespoon olive oil
4 lamb neck chops (680g), trimmed
1 large brown onion (200g), chopped finely
2 cloves garlic, crushed
410g (13 ounces) canned diced tomatoes
½ cup (125ml) water
8 baby brown onions (200g)
500g (1 pound) baby new potatoes, halved
400g (12½ ounces) baby carrots,
    trimmed, peeled
1 cup (120g) frozen peas
2 tablespoons coarsely chopped
    fresh flat-leaf parsley

1 Heat oil in 6-litre (24-cup) pressure cooker;
cook lamb, in batches, until browned. Remove
from cooker.
2 Cook chopped onion and garlic in cooker,
stirring, until onion softens. Return lamb to
cooker with undrained tomatoes and the water;
secure lid. Bring cooker to high pressure.
Reduce heat to stabilise pressure; cook
15 minutes.
3 Meanwhile, peel baby onions, leaving root
ends intact.
4 Release cooker pressure using the quick
release method (page 5); remove lid. Stir in
potato and onions, top with carrots; secure lid.
Bring cooker to high pressure. Reduce heat to
stabilise pressure; cook 5 minutes.
5 Release pressure using the quick release
method (page 5); remove lid. Add peas;
simmer, uncovered, until peas are tender.
Season to taste. Serve sprinkled with parsley.

tips If you have an electric pressure cooker you won't
need to reduce the heat to stabilise pressure, your
cooker will automatically stabilise itself. Always check
with the manufacturer's instructions before using.
Recipe not suitable to freeze.

LAMB

CASSOULET

prep + cook time **1 hour 15 minutes** serves **8**
nutritional count per serving **44.1g total fat (15.8g
saturated fat); 2913kJ (697 cal); 24.6g carbohydrate;
46.4g protein; 9.6g fibre**

1½ cups (300g) dried white beans
500g (1 pound) boneless pork belly, rind on
1 dried bay leaf
1.25 litres (5 cups) water
2 tablespoons olive oil
4 toulouse sausages (480g)
4 lamb neck chops (680g), trimmed
150g (4½ ounces) speck, chopped finely
1 large brown onion (200g), chopped finely
4 cloves garlic, crushed
410g (13 ounces) canned diced tomatoes
2 tablespoons tomato paste
1 cup (70g) fresh breadcrumbs
2 tablespoons finely chopped
    fresh flat-leaf parsley
1 clove garlic, crushed, extra

1 Combine beans, pork, bay leaf and the water
in 6-litre (24-cup) pressure cooker; secure lid.
Bring cooker to high pressure. Reduce heat
to stabilise pressure; cook 30 minutes.
2 Release pressure using the quick release
method (page 5); remove lid. Strain pork
mixture over large heatproof bowl. Discard
bay leaf; reserve pork, beans and cooking
liquid separately.

3 Heat half the oil in cooker; cook sausages
until browned. Remove from cooker. Cook
lamb in cooker until browned. Remove from
cooker. Cook speck in cooker, stirring, until
browned. Add onion and garlic; cook, stirring,
until onion softens. Return lamb, sausages,
pork and beans to cooker with undrained
tomatoes, paste and 1½ cups (375ml) of the
reserved cooking liquid; secure lid. Bring
cooker to high pressure. Reduce heat to
stabilise pressure; cook 20 minutes.
4 Release pressure using the quick release
method (page 5); remove lid. Remove pork,
lamb and sausages. Secure lid of cooker;
bring cooker to high pressure. Reduce heat
to stabilise pressure; cook 5 minutes.
5 Meanwhile, coarsely chop pork and
sausages; discard bones from lamb, chop
meat coarsely.
6 Release cooker pressure using quick
release method (page 5); remove lid. Return
meat to cooker; simmer, uncovered, until hot.
Season to taste.
7 Heat remaining oil in medium frying pan;
cook breadcrumbs, stirring, until browned
and crisp. Stir in parsley and extra garlic.
Transfer cassoulet to serving dish; sprinkle
with breadcrumb mixture.

tips **If you have an electric pressure cooker you won't
need to reduce the heat to stabilise pressure, your
cooker will automatically stabilise itself. Always check
with the manufacturer's instructions before using. We
used cannellini beans for this recipe but you can also
use lima or haricot beans. Recipe suitable to freeze.**

LAMB ROGAN JOSH

prep + cook time **45 minutes** serves **4**
nutritional count per serving 38.1g total fat (12.2g
saturated fat); 2378kJ (569 cal); 14.3g carbohydrate;
37.8g protein; 9.3g fibre

2 tablespoons ghee
800g (1½ pounds) lamb neck chops, trimmed
2 large brown onions (400g), chopped finely
4 cloves garlic, crushed
½ cup (150g) rogan josh curry paste
410g (13 ounces) canned tomato puree
¼ cup (60ml) water
250g (8 ounces) spinach, trimmed,
    chopped coarsely
½ cup coarsely chopped fresh coriander
    (cilantro)

1 Heat half the ghee in 6-litre (24-cup)
pressure cooker; cook lamb, in batches, until
browned. Remove from cooker.
2 Heat remaining ghee in cooker; cook onion,
stirring, until browned lightly. Add garlic; cook,
stirring, until fragrant. Return lamb to cooker
with paste, puree and the water; secure lid.
Bring cooker to high pressure. Reduce heat
to stabilise pressure; cook 25 minutes.
3 Release pressure using the quick release
method (page 5); remove lid. Stir in spinach
and coriander; season to taste.

tips If you have an electric pressure cooker you won't
need to reduce the heat to stabilise pressure, your
cooker will automatically stabilise itself. Always check
with the manufacturer's instructions before using.
Recipe suitable to freeze.
serving suggestion Serve with steamed basmati rice,
pappadums and raita.

SPICY LAMB IN TOMATO AND SPINACH SAUCE

prep + cook time **40 minutes** serves **4**
nutritional count per serving **18.5g total fat (6.6g**
saturated fat); 1789kJ (428 cal); 5.8g carbohydrate;
57.8g protein; 2.9g fibre

1 tablespoon vegetable oil
1kg (2 pounds) boned lamb leg,
   chopped coarsely
1 medium brown onion (150g),
   chopped finely
3 cloves garlic, crushed
2 fresh small red thai (serrano) chillies,
   chopped finely
2 teaspoons each ground coriander and
   garam masala
1 teaspoon each ground cumin and
   ground fenugreek
½ teaspoon ground turmeric
410g (13 ounces) canned crushed tomatoes
½ cup (125ml) beef stock
100g (3 ounces) baby spinach leaves,
   shredded finely
2 tablespoons finely chopped fresh
   coriander (cilantro)

1 Heat half the oil in 6-litre (24-cup) pressure
cooker; cook lamb, in batches, until browned.
Remove from cooker.
2 Heat remaining oil in cooker; cook onion,
garlic and chilli, stirring, until onion softens.
Add spices; cook, stirring, until fragrant.
Return lamb to cooker with undrained tomatoes
and stock; secure lid. Bring cooker to high
pressure. Reduce heat to stabilise pressure;
cook 25 minutes.
3 Release pressure using the quick release
method (page 5); remove lid. Stir in spinach
and coriander; season to taste.

tips If you have an electric pressure cooker you won't
need to reduce the heat to stabilise pressure, your
cooker will automatically stabilise itself. Always check
with the manufacturer's instructions before using.
Recipe suitable to freeze.
serving suggestion Serve with steamed basmati rice
and warm naan.

LEMON AND GINGER LAMB SHANKS WITH BROAD BEANS

prep + cook time **50 minutes** serves **4**
nutritional count per serving **21.5g total fat (9g
saturated fat); 1952kJ (467 cal); 26.5g carbohydrate;
36.4g protein; 11.5g fibre**

1 tablespoon olive oil
4 french-trimmed lamb shanks (1kg)
1 large brown onion (200g), chopped finely
3 cloves garlic, crushed
2 tablespoons thinly sliced preserved
  lemon rind
5cm (2-inch) piece fresh ginger (25g), grated
1 cinnamon stick
¼ cup (60ml) lemon juice
½ cup (125ml) water
300g (9½ ounces) frozen broad beans
  (fava beans)
600g (1¼ pounds) kipfler (fingerling)
  potatoes, halved
20g (¾ ounce) butter
1 cup finely chopped fresh coriander
  (cilantro)
½ cup finely chopped fresh flat-leaf parsley

1 Heat half the oil in 6-litre (24-cup) pressure
cooker; cook lamb, in batches, until browned.
Remove from cooker.
2 Heat remaining oil in cooker; cook onion
and garlic, stirring, until onion softens. Add
preserved lemon, ginger and cinnamon;
cook, stirring, until fragrant. Return lamb to
cooker with juice and the water; secure lid.
Bring cooker to high pressure. Reduce heat
to stabilise pressure; cook 25 minutes.
3 Meanwhile, cook beans in large saucepan
of boiling water about 2 minutes or until tender;
drain. Rinse under cold water; drain. Peel away
grey skins.
4 Release pressure using the quick release
method (page 5); remove lid. Add potato;
secure lid. Bring cooker to high pressure. Reduce
heat to stabilise pressure; cook 10 minutes.
5 Meanwhile, melt butter in medium frying pan;
cook herbs, stirring, until bright green.
6 Release cooker pressure using the quick
release method (page 5); remove lid. Stir in
beans and herbs; simmer, uncovered until hot.
Season to taste.

tips If you have an electric pressure cooker you won't
need to reduce the heat to stabilise pressure, your
cooker will automatically stabilise itself. Always check
with the manufacturer's instructions before using.
Preserved lemons, a prominent ingredient in North
African cooking, are salted lemons bottled for several
months; the flavour is salty, unique and perfumed.
To use, discard flesh, rinse well, using the rind only.
This recipe is not suitable to freeze.

LAMB AND APRICOT TAGINE

prep + cook time **40 minutes** serves **6**
nutritional count per serving **21.3g total fat (7.5g
saturated fat); 1526kJ (365 cal); 7.2g carbohydrate;
35g protein; 2.6g fibre**

1 tablespoon olive oil
1kg (2 pounds) boned lamb shoulder,
   trimmed, chopped coarsely
1 medium brown onion (150g), sliced thinly
2 cloves garlic, crushed
1 teaspoon each ground coriander, cumin
   and cinnamon
¾ cup (180ml) beef stock
½ cup (75g) coarsely chopped dried apricots
100g (3 ounces) baby spinach leaves
¼ cup (35g) roasted slivered almonds

1 Heat half the oil in 6-litre (24-cup) pressure
cooker; cook lamb, in batches, until browned.
Remove from cooker.
2 Heat remaining oil in cooker; cook onion and
garlic, stirring, until onion softens. Add spices;
cook, stirring, until fragrant. Return lamb to
cooker with stock; secure lid. Bring cooker
to high pressure. Reduce heat to stabilise
pressure; cook 25 minutes.
3 Release pressure using the quick release
method (page 5); remove lid. Add apricots;
secure lid. Bring cooker to high pressure.
Reduce heat to stabilise pressure; cook
2 minutes. Release pressure using the quick
release method (page 5); remove lid. Stir in
spinach; season to taste. Serve tagine
sprinkled with nuts.

tips If you have an electric pressure cooker you won't
need to reduce the heat to stabilise pressure, your
cooker will automatically stabilise itself. Always check
with the manufacturer's instructions before using.
Recipe suitable to freeze.
serving suggestion **Serve with couscous.**

HOT-PEPPERED LAMB CURRY

prep + cook time **1 hour** serves **4**
nutritional count per serving 17.7g total fat (9.7g saturated fat); 1442kJ (345 cal); 8.6g carbohydrate; 36.5g protein; 3g fibre

2 fresh long green chillies
2 tablespoons ghee
600g (1¼ pounds) boned lamb leg, chopped coarsely
2 large brown onions (400g), sliced thinly
3 cloves garlic, crushed
4cm (1½-inch) piece fresh ginger (20g), grated
3 cloves
4 green cardamom pods, bruised
2 cinnamon sticks
2 teaspoons coarsely cracked black pepper
2 medium tomatoes (300g), chopped finely
¼ cup (70g) yogurt
½ cup (125ml) water
¼ cup (60ml) lemon juice
⅓ cup finely chopped fresh coriander (cilantro)

1 Finely chop one of the chillies; finely shred remaining chilli.
2 Heat half the ghee in 6-litre (24-cup) pressure cooker; cook lamb, in batches, until browned. Remove from cooker.
3 Heat remaining ghee in same cooker; cook onion, stirring, about 5 minutes or until browned lightly. Add garlic and ginger; cook, stirring, until fragrant. Return lamb to cooker with spices, tomato, chopped chilli, yogurt and the water; secure lid. Bring cooker to high pressure. Reduce heat to stabilise pressure; cook 25 minutes.
4 Release pressure using the quick release method (page 5); remove lid. Stir in juice; season to taste. Serve sprinkled with coriander and shredded chilli, if you like.

tips If you have an electric pressure cooker you won't need to reduce the heat to stabilise pressure, your cooker will automatically stabilise itself. Always check with the manufacturer's instructions before using.
This is a hot curry. If you prefer a milder version, reduce the amount of pepper and chilli. You can also serve it with an extra dollop of yogurt if you like.
Recipe suitable to freeze.
serving suggestion **Serve with steamed white rice.**

COUNTRY LAMB AND BARLEY STEW

prep + cook time **40 minutes** serves **6**
nutritional count per serving **13.1g total fat (4.7g
saturated fat); 1747kJ (418 cal); 29.2g carbohydrate;
42.5g protein; 6g fibre**

2 tablespoons plain (all-purpose) flour
1kg (2 pounds) boned lamb leg,
    chopped coarsely
1 tablespoon olive oil
8 baby brown onions (200g)
2 cups (500ml) chicken stock
⅔ cup (130g) pearl barley
3 sprigs fresh thyme
2 stalks celery (300g), trimmed,
    chopped coarsely
2 medium carrots (240g), chopped coarsely
400g (12½ ounces) baby new potatoes,
    quartered

1 Season flour in large bowl; add lamb, toss
to coat in flour. Shake off excess. Heat half
the oil in 6-litre (24-cup) pressure cooker;
cook lamb, in batches, until browned.
Remove from cooker.
2 Meanwhile, peel onions, leaving root ends
intact; halve.
3 Heat remaining oil in cooker; cook onion,
stirring, until browned lightly. Remove from
cooker. Return lamb to cooker with stock,
barley and thyme; secure lid. Bring cooker
to high pressure. Reduce heat to stabilise
pressure; cook 20 minutes.
4 Release pressure using the quick release
method (page 5); remove lid. Add onion,
celery, carrot and potato; secure lid. Bring
cooker to high pressure. Reduce heat to
stabilise pressure; cook lamb and vegetable
mixture 7 minutes.
5 Release pressure using the quick release
method (page 5); remove lid. Season to taste.
Serve sprinkled with extra thyme leaves,
if you like.

tips **If you have an electric pressure cooker you won't
need to reduce the heat to stabilise pressure, your
cooker will automatically stabilise itself. Always check
with the manufacturer's instructions before using.
Recipe suitable to freeze.**
serving suggestion **Serve with crusty bread.**

BRAISED LAMB SHANKS WITH MUSHROOM RISOTTO

prep + cook time **50 minutes** serves **6**
nutritional count per serving **25.1g total fat (10.6g
saturated fat); 2353kJ (563 cal); 43.8g carbohydrate;
35.5g protein; 3.1g fibre**

2 tablespoons olive oil
6 french-trimmed lamb shanks (1.5kg)
3 stalks celery (450g), untrimmed, halved
1 medium leek (350g), trimmed, halved
3 stalks fresh rosemary
3 cloves garlic, bruised
1 litre (4 cups) water
⅔ cup (20g) mixed dried mushrooms
1 large brown onion (200g), chopped finely
1½ cups (300g) arborio rice
½ cup (125ml) dry white wine
½ cup (40g) finely grated parmesan cheese
30g (1 ounce) butter, chopped finely

1 Heat half the oil in 6-litre (24-cup) pressure cooker; cook lamb, in batches, until browned. Remove from cooker.
2 Return lamb to cooker with celery, leek, rosemary, garlic and the water; secure lid. Bring cooker to high pressure. Reduce heat to stabilise pressure; cook 30 minutes.
3 Release pressure using the quick release method (page 5); remove lid. Strain over large heatproof bowl; cover shanks to keep warm. Discard vegetables. Reserve 3½ cups (875ml) cooking liquid; add dried mushrooms.
4 Heat remaining oil in cooker; cook onion, stirring, until soft. Add rice; stir to coat in onion mixture. Stir in wine and cooking liquid with mushrooms; secure lid. Bring cooker to high pressure. Reduce heat to stabilise pressure; cook 7 minutes.
5 Release pressure using the quick release method (page 5); remove lid. Stand, covered, 5 minutes or until liquid is absorbed. Stir in cheese and butter; season to taste. Sprinkle risotto with a little extra rosemary and grated parmesan; serve with shanks.

tips If you have an electric pressure cooker you won't need to reduce the heat to stabilise pressure, your cooker will automatically stabilise itself. Always check with the manufacturer's instructions before using. Covering the shanks with the cooked celery and leek is an easy way to keep the lamb hot and moist while you cook the risotto. Recipe not suitable to freeze.

BEST-EVER BOLOGNESE

prep + cook time 45 minutes makes 6 cups
nutritional count per 1 cup 12.2g total fat (3.8g
saturated fat); 1129kJ (270 cal); 7.2g carbohydrate;
28.2g protein; 2.8g fibre

1 tablespoon olive oil
1 medium brown onion (150g),
  chopped finely
2 cloves garlic, crushed
750g (1½ pounds) minced (ground)
  pork and veal
⅓ cup (95g) tomato paste
800g (1½ pounds) canned crushed tomatoes
½ cup (125ml) dry red wine
2 tablespoons each finely chopped fresh
  flat-leaf parsley and oregano

1 Heat oil in 6-litre (24-cup) pressure cooker;
add onion and garlic; cook, stirring, until onion
softens. Add pork and veal; cook, stirring, until
browned. Add paste, undrained tomatoes and
wine to cooker; secure lid. Bring cooker to high
pressure. Reduce heat to stabilise pressure;
cook 20 minutes.
2 Release pressure using the quick release
method (page 5); remove lid. Simmer,
uncovered, about 10 minutes or until sauce
thickens slightly. Stir in herbs; season to taste.

tips If you have an electric pressure cooker you won't
need to reduce the heat to stabilise pressure, your
cooker will automatically stabilise itself. Always check
with the manufacturer's instructions before using.
Recipe suitable to freeze.
serving suggestion Cook 500g (1 pound) dry spaghetti
for enough pasta to serve with this sauce. Leftover
sauce can be used to make lasagne or served over
roasted jacket potatoes.

PORK

BRAZILIAN FEIJOADA

prep + cook time **1 hour** serves **8**
nutritional count per serving **41.8g total fat (11.7g saturated fat); 2529kJ (605 cal); 7.4g carbohydrate; 45.5g protein; 11.2g fibre**

600g (1¼ pounds) boneless pork belly, rind on
600g (1¼ pounds) american-style pork spare ribs
2 cups (400g) dried black (turtle) beans
2 dried bay leaves
1.5 litres (6 cups) water
2 tablespoons olive oil
150g (4½ ounces) speck, chopped finely
1 large brown onion (200g), chopped finely
5 cloves garlic, crushed
1 cured chorizo sausage (170g)
2 tablespoons coarsely chopped fresh flat-leaf parsley

1 Chop pork belly coarsely, cut ribs into serving sized pieces.

2 Combine beans, pork belly, ribs, bay leaves and the water in 6-litre (24-cup) pressure cooker; secure lid. Bring cooker to high pressure. Reduce heat to stabilise pressure; cook 35 minutes.

3 Release pressure using the quick release method (page 5); remove lid. Strain over large heatproof bowl. Reserve 2 cups (500ml) cooking liquid; reserve bay leaves.

4 Heat oil in cooker; cook speck and reserved bay leaves, stirring, until speck is browned. Add onion and garlic; cook, stirring, until onion softens. Return beans, pork belly and ribs to cooker with whole chorizo and reserved cooking liquid; secure lid. Bring cooker to high pressure. Reduce heat to stabilise pressure; cook 10 minutes.

5 Release pressure using the quick release method (page 5); remove lid. Remove chorizo; chop coarsely, return to cooker. Season to taste. Serve sprinkled with parsley

tips If you have an electric pressure cooker you won't need to reduce the heat to stabilise pressure, your cooker will automatically stabilise itself. Always check with the manufacturer's instructions before using. Recipe suitable to freeze. Feijoada is traditionally a Portuguese dish made with red kidney beans. Its name comes from "feijõa", Portuguese for beans. Imported to Brazil (a former Portuguese colony), feijoada, pronounced "fey-ju-arda" has become over time their national dish. It usually contains pigs' ears and trotters and is served sprinkled with farofa (roasted cassava flour).
serving suggestion **Serve with steamed rice.**

STICKY PORK SPARE RIBS

prep + cook time **30 minutes** serves **4**
nutritional count per serving **13.6g total fat (4.6g
saturated fat); 1484kJ (355 cal); 20.2g carbohydrate;
37.2g protein; 1g fibre**

1.5kg (3 pounds) american-style pork
    spare ribs
1 cup (250ml) water
⅓ cup (115g) orange marmalade
⅓ cup (80ml) kecap manis
4 cloves garlic, crushed
8cm (3¼-inch) piece fresh ginger (40g),
    grated
2 teaspoons five-spice powder

1 Combine ribs and the water in 6-litre
(24-cup) pressure cooker; secure lid. Bring
cooker to high pressure. Reduce heat to
stabilise pressure; cook 15 minutes.
2 Meanwhile, combine remaining ingredients
in large bowl. Preheat grill (broiler).
3 Release cooker pressure using the quick
release method (page 5); remove lid. Drain ribs;
combine with marmalade mixture. Place ribs,
in single layer, on oiled wire rack over large
shallow baking dish filled with 1cm (½ inch)
water. Grill ribs about 8 minutes or until
browned, turning halfway through cooking
time and brushing occasionally with remaining
marmalade mixture.

tips If you have an electric pressure cooker you won't
need to reduce the heat to stabilise pressure, your
cooker will automatically stabilise itself. Always check
with the manufacturer's instructions before using.
Recipe not suitable to freeze.

HOISIN PORK WITH SALTED CRACKLING

prep + cook time **50 minutes** serves **6**

nutritional count per serving 45.9g total fat (15.4g saturated fat); 2521kJ (603 cal); 9.9g carbohydrate; 37.6g protein; 3.2g fibre

1.2kg (2½ pounds) boneless pork belly, rind on
1 cinnamon stick
2 star anise
⅓ cup (120g) hoisin sauce
5cm (2-inch) strip orange rind
½ cup (125ml) orange juice
½ cup (125ml) water
1 tablespoon fine cooking salt
500g (1 pound) choy sum, trimmed

1 Using small sharp knife, score pork rind at shallow 1cm (½-inch) intervals.
2 Combine cinnamon, star anise, sauce, rind, juice and the water in 6-litre (24-cup) pressure cooker. Place pork, rind-side up, on oiled wire rack in cooker; secure lid. Bring cooker to high pressure. Reduce heat to stabilise pressure; cook 30 minutes.
3 Release pressure using the quick release method (page 5); remove lid. Remove pork from cooker; strain cooking liquid into small saucepan.
4 Preheat griller (broiler). Place pork, rind-side up, on wire rack over large shallow baking dish; sprinkle rind with salt. Grill pork about 10 minutes or until crackling is browned lightly and crisp.
5 Meanwhile, bring reserved cooking liquid to the boil. Boil, uncovered, about 5 minutes or until sauce thickens slightly. Add choy sum, cook until wilted.
6 Cut pork into six pieces. Serve pork with sauce and choy sum.

tips If you have an electric pressure cooker you won't need to reduce the heat to stabilise pressure, your cooker will automatically stabilise itself. Always check with the manufacturer's instructions before using. Recipe not suitable to freeze.

PORK, FENNEL AND OLIVE RAGOUT

prep + cook time **45 minutes** serves **4**
nutritional count per serving 25.2g total fat (7.5g saturated fat); 2149kJ (514 cal); 11.2g carbohydrate; 55.7g protein; 3.4g fibre

2 tablespoons plain (all-purpose) flour
1kg (2 pounds) pork neck, chopped coarsely
1 tablespoon olive oil
1 medium leek (350g), sliced thinly
1 medium fennel bulb (300g), trimmed,
    sliced thinly
2 cloves garlic, crushed
$\frac{1}{3}$ cup (80ml) dry white wine
$\frac{1}{2}$ cup (125ml) chicken stock
2 tablespoons white balsamic vinegar
$\frac{1}{2}$ cup (60g) seeded mixed olives
2 tablespoons coarsely chopped fresh
    flat-leaf parsley

1 Season flour in large bowl; add pork, toss to coat in flour. Shake off excess. Heat half the oil in 6-litre (24-cup) pressure cooker; cook pork, in batches, until browned. Remove from cooker.
2 Heat remaining oil in cooker; cook leek, fennel and garlic, stirring, until vegetables soften. Return pork to cooker with wine, stock and vinegar; secure lid. Bring cooker to high pressure. Reduce heat to stabilise pressure; cook 30 minutes.
3 Release pressure using the quick release method (page 5); remove lid. Stir in olives; season to taste. Serve sprinkled with parsley.

tips If you have an electric pressure cooker you won't need to reduce the heat to stabilise pressure, your cooker will automatically stabilise itself. Always check with the manufacturer's instructions before using. Recipe suitable to freeze.

ALLSPICE also called pimento or jamaican pepper; tastes of nutmeg, cumin, clove and cinnamon. Available whole or ground.

ALMONDS, SLIVERED small pieces of almond cut lengthways.

BARLEY a nutritious grain used in soups and stews. Hulled barley, the least processed, is high in fibre. Pearl barley has had the husk removed then been steamed and polished so that only the "pearl" of the grain remains.

BAY LEAVES aromatic leaves from the bay tree available fresh or dried; adds a peppery flavour.

BEANS

black (turtle) also called black kidney beans; an earthy-flavoured dried bean completely different from the better-known chinese black beans (fermented soybeans).

broad (fava) also called windsor and horse beans; available dried, fresh, canned and frozen. Fresh should be peeled twice (discarding both the outer long green pod and the beige-green tough inner shell); frozen beans have had their pods removed but the beige shell still needs to be removed.

cannellini small white bean similar in appearance and flavour to other varieties (great northern, navy or haricot). Available dried or canned.

kidney medium-size red bean, slightly floury in texture yet sweet in flavour; sold dried or canned.

white a generic term we use for canned or dried cannellini, haricot, navy or great northern beans.

BEEF

blade taken from the shoulder; isn't as tender as other cuts so needs slow cooking for best results.

cheek the cheek muscle. A very tough and lean cut of meat; often used for braising or slow cooking to produce a tender result.

chuck inexpensive cut from the neck and shoulder area; good minced and slow-cooked.

corned also known as corned silverside; little fat, cut from the upper leg and cured. Sold cryovac-packed in brine.

gravy boneless stewing beef from shin; slow-cooked, imbues stocks, soups and casseroles with a gelatine richness. Cut crossways, with bone in, is osso buco.

CAPERS the grey-green buds of a warm climate shrub, sold either dried and salted or pickled in a vinegar brine; tiny young ones, called baby capers, are available bottled in brine or dried in salt.

CAPSICUM (BELL PEPPER) also called pepper. Discard seeds and membranes before use.

CARDAMOM a spice native to India and used extensively in its cuisine; can be purchased in the pod, as seeds or ground.

CHICKEN

drumstick leg with skin and bone intact.

maryland leg and thigh connected in a single piece; bones and skin intact.

thigh cutlet thigh with skin and bone intact; sometimes found skinned with bone intact.

thigh fillet thigh with skin and bone removed.

CHICKPEAS (GARBANZO BEANS) also called hummus or channa; an irregularly round, sandy-coloured legume used extensively in Mediterranean, Indian and Hispanic cooking. Firm texture even after

cooking, a floury mouth-feel and robust nutty flavour; available canned or dried (soak for several hours in cold water before use).

CHILLIES use rubber gloves when handling fresh chillies as they can burn your skin. We use unseeded chillies because seeds contain the heat; use fewer chillies rather than seed the lot.

cayenne pepper a long, extremely hot, dried, ground red chilli native to South America.

chipotle pronounced cheh-pot-lay. Dried and smoked jalapeño chilli. Has a deep, intensely smoky flavour, the chipotle is dark brown in colour and wrinkled in appearance.

flakes also sold as crushed chilli; dehydrated deep-red extremely fine slices and whole seeds.

jalapeño pronounced hah-lah-pen-yo. Fairly hot, medium-sized, plump, green chilli; available pickled, sold canned or bottled, and fresh.

long green any unripened chilli.

long red available both fresh and dried; a generic term used for a moderately hot, long, thin chilli.

red thai (serrano) also called "scuds" or "bird's eye" chillies; tiny, very hot and bright red.

CHORIZO small, coarsely-ground pork sausages, Spanish in origin. They are deeply smoked, very spicy and dry-cured so they don't need cooking. Can also be purchased as fresh sausages.

CHOY SUM a member of the buk choy family; easy to identify with its long stems and yellow flowers.

COCONUT CREAM obtained from the first pressing of the coconut flesh alone, without the addition of water; the second pressing (less rich) is coconut milk. Available canned or dried.

GLOSSARY

CORIANDER (CILANTRO) also called pak chee or chinese parsley; bright-green-leafed herb with both pungent aroma and taste. Coriander seeds are dried and sold either whole or ground.

CORNFLOUR (CORNSTARCH) available made from corn or wheat; used for thickening.

CREAM

pouring also called pure or fresh cream. It has no additives; contains a minimum fat content of 35%.

thickened (heavy) a whipping cream that contains a thickener. It has a minimum fat content of 35%.

EGGS we use large chicken eggs weighing an average of 60g unless stated otherwise in the recipes in this book. If a recipe calls for raw or barely cooked eggs, exercise caution if there is a salmonella problem in your area, particularly in food eaten by children and pregnant women.

FISH SAUCE called naam pla on the label if Thai-made, nuoc naam if Vietnamese; the two are almost identical. Made from pulverised salted fermented fish; has a pungent smell and taste.

FIVE-SPICE POWDER also known as chinese five-spice. Although the ingredients do vary it is usually a fragrant mixture of ground cinnamon, cloves, star anise, sichuan pepper and fennel seeds.

FLOUR

plain (all-purpose) unbleached wheat flour, it is the best for baking: the gluten content ensures a strong dough, for a light result.

self-raising all-purpose plain or wholemeal flour with baking powder and salt added; make at home in the proportion of 1 cup flour to 2 teaspoons baking powder.

GALANGAL also called lengkaus or ka if fresh and laos if dried and powdered; a root, similar to ginger with a hot-sour citrusy flavour.

GARAM MASALA literally meaning blended spices in its northern Indian place of origin; cardamom, cloves, cinnamon, coriander, fennel and cumin, roasted and ground together.

GHEE clarified butter; with the milk solids removed, this fat has a high smoking point so can be heated to a high temperature without burning. Used in Indian recipes.

GINGER

fresh also called green or root ginger; the gnarled root of a tropical plant.

ground also called powdered ginger; used as a flavouring in baking but cannot be substituted for fresh ginger.

HOISIN SAUCE a thick, sweet and spicy chinese barbecue sauce made from fermented soybeans, onions and garlic; used as a marinade or baste.

KAFFIR LIME LEAVES also known as bai magrood and looks like two glossy dark green leaves joined end to end. Sold fresh, dried or frozen; fresh lime peel may be substituted.

KECAP MANIS a dark, thick, sweet soy sauce used in South-East Asian cuisines.

KUMARA (ORANGE SWEET POTATO) the Polynesian name of an orange-fleshed sweet potato often confused with yam; good baked, boiled, mashed or fried.

LAMB

leg cut from the hindquarter; can be boned, butterflied, rolled and tied, or cut into dice.

minced ground lamb.

neck chops chops cut from the neck, ideal for stewing, braising and making stock.

shanks, french-trimmed also called drumsticks or frenched shanks. The gristle and bone end are discarded and the meat trimmed.

shoulder large, tasty piece with much connective tissue so is best pot-roasted or braised. Can be cut into dice and makes good mince.

LEMON GRASS also called takrai, serai or serah. A lemon-scented, aromatic tropical grass; the white lower part of the stem is used.

LENTILS (red, brown, yellow) dried pulses often identified by and named after their colour.

MAPLE SYRUP distilled from the sap of sugar maple trees found only in Canada and the USA. Maple-flavoured syrup is not a substitute.

MARSALA a fortified Italian wine recognisable by its intense amber colour and complex aroma.

MUSHROOMS, BUTTON small, cultivated white mushrooms with a mild flavour. If mushroom type is unspecified, always use button mushrooms.

OIL

olive made from ripened olives. Extra virgin and virgin are the first and second press, respectively, of the olives and are therefore considered the best; the apellation "light" refers to taste not fat levels.

peanut pressed from ground peanuts; the most commonly used oil in Asian cooking for its capacity to handle high heat without burning.

vegetable any of a number of oils sourced from plant rather than animal fats.

ONIONS

baby also called pickling onions and cocktail onions; baby brown onions, larger than shallots.

brown and white these onions are interchangeable; white onions have a more pungent flesh.

green (scallion) also called (incorrectly) shallot; an immature onion picked before the bulb has formed, with a white base and a long, green edible stalk.

red also known as spanish, red spanish or bermuda onion; a sweet, large, purple-red onion.

shallots also called french shallots, golden shallots or eschalots; small brown-skinned elongated members of the onion family.

PANCETTA an Italian unsmoked bacon, pork belly cured in salt and spices then rolled into a sausage shape and dried for several weeks.

PAPRIKA ground dried red capsicum (bell pepper); available sweet, hot, mild and smoked.

PISTACHIOS delicately flavoured green nuts inside hard shells. We always use shelled nuts.

POLENTA also called cornmeal; a flour-like cereal made of dried corn (maize). Also the dish made from it.

PORK

american-style spareribs trimmed mid-loin ribs.

belly fatty cut sold in rashers or in a piece, with or without rind or bone.

fillet skinless, boneless eye-fillet cut from the loin.

ham hock the lower portion of the leg; includes the meat, fat and bone. Most have been cured and smoked.

neck sometimes called pork scotch, boneless cut from the foreloin.

speck smoked pork.

POTATOES

baby new also called chats; not a separate variety but an early harvest with very thin skin. Serve unpeeled steamed, or in salads.

coliban round, smooth white skin and flesh; good for baking and mashing.

kipfler (fingerling) small, finger-shaped, nutty flavour; great baked and in salads.

sebago white skin, oval; good fried, mashed and baked.

PRESERVED LEMON whole or quartered salted, preserved lemons. Use the rind only and rinse well under cold water before using.

QUINCE yellow-skinned fruit with hard texture and tart taste; long cooking makes the flesh deep pink.

RICE

arborio small, round grain rice well-suited to absorb a large amount of liquid; the high level of starch makes it especially suitable for risottos, giving the dish its classic creaminess.

long-grain elongated grains that remain separate when cooked.

SAFFRON stigma of a member of the crocus family, available ground or in strands; imparts a yellow-orange colour to food once infused.

SILVER BEET (SWISS CHARD)

also known, incorrectly, as spinach; has fleshy stalks and large leaves, both of which can be prepared as for spinach.

SPINACH also known as english spinach and incorrectly, silver beet.

STAR ANISE dried star-shaped pod with an astringent aniseed flavour; used to flavour stocks and marinades. Available whole and ground.

SUGAR

caster (superfine) also known as finely granulated table sugar.

dark brown a moist, dark brown sugar with a rich, distinctive full flavour from molasses syrup.

light brown a very soft, finely granulated sugar that retains molasses for its colour and flavour.

palm also called nam tan pip, jaggery, jawa or gula melaka; made from the sap of the sugar palm tree. Use brown sugar if unavailable.

TOMATOES

bottled pasta sauce a prepared tomato-based sauce (sometimes called ragu or sugo); comes in varying degrees of thickness and with different flavourings.

canned whole peeled tomatoes in natural juices; available crushed, chopped or diced. Use tomatoes undrained unless stated otherwise.

paste triple-concentrated tomato puree used to flavour soups, stews and sauces.

puree canned pureed tomatoes; substitute with fresh peeled and pureed tomatoes.

TOULOUSE SAUSAGE essential ingredient of a French cassoulet, a garlic and herb-laden coarse sausage.

TURMERIC also called kamin; is a rhizome related to galangal and ginger. Must be grated or pounded to release its aroma and flavour. Fresh can be substituted with dried powder.

VEAL, SHIN gelatinous shin meat of a beef calf; sold thickly sliced and with bone-in as osso buco.

YOGURT we use plain full-cream yogurt unless stated otherwise.

ZUCCHINI also called courgette; small, pale- or dark-green or yellow vegetable of the squash family. Its edible flowers can be stuffed.

CONVERSION CHART

MEASURES

One Australian metric measuring cup holds approximately 250ml, one Australian metric tablespoon holds 20ml, one Australian metric teaspoon holds 5ml.

The difference between one country's measuring cups and another's is within a 2- or 3-teaspoon variance, and will not affect your cooking results. North America, New Zealand and the United Kingdom use a 15ml tablespoon. All cup and spoon measurements are level. The most accurate way of measuring dry ingredients is to weigh them. When measuring liquids, use a clear glass or plastic jug with metric markings.

We use large eggs with an average weight of 60g.

DRY MEASURES

METRIC	IMPERIAL
15g	½oz
30g	1oz
60g	2oz
90g	3oz
125g	4oz (¼lb)
155g	5oz
185g	6oz
220g	7oz
250g	8oz (½lb)
280g	9oz
315g	10oz
345g	11oz
375g	12oz (¾lb)
410g	13oz
440g	14oz
470g	15oz
500g	16oz (1lb)
750g	24oz (1½lb)
1kg	32oz (2lb)

LIQUID MEASURES

METRIC	IMPERIAL
30ml	1 fluid oz
60ml	2 fluid oz
100ml	3 fluid oz
125ml	4 fluid oz
150ml	5 fluid oz
190ml	6 fluid oz
250ml	8 fluid oz
300ml	10 fluid oz
500ml	16 fluid oz
600ml	20 fluid oz
1000ml (1 litre)	1¾ pints

LENGTH MEASURES

METRIC	IMPERIAL
3mm	⅛in
6mm	¼in
1cm	½in
2cm	¾in
2.5cm	1in
5cm	2in
6cm	2½in
8cm	3in
10cm	4in
13cm	5in
15cm	6in
18cm	7in
20cm	8in
23cm	9in
25cm	10in
28cm	11in
30cm	12in (1ft)

OVEN TEMPERATURES

The oven temperatures in this book are for conventional ovens; if you have a fan-forced oven, decrease the temperature by 10-20 degrees.

	°C (CELSIUS)	°F (FAHRENHEIT)
Very slow	120	250
Slow	150	300
Moderately slow	160	325
Moderate	180	350
Moderately hot	200	400
Hot	220	425
Very hot	240	475

The imperial measurements used in these recipes are approximate only. Measurements for cake pans are approximate only. Using same-shaped cake pans of a similar size should not affect the outcome of your baking. We measure the inside top of the cake pan to determine sizes.

INDEX

Published in 2012 by ACP Books, Sydney

ACP Books are published by ACP Magazines Limited,
a division of Nine Entertainment Co.

54 Park St, Sydney;

GPO Box 4088, Sydney, NSW 2001, Australia

phone (+61) 2 9282 8618; fax (+61) 2 9126 3702

acpbooks@acpmagazines.com.au; www.acpbooks.com.au

ACP BOOKS

General Manager - Christine Whiston

Editor-in-Chief - Susan Tomnay

Creative Director - Hieu Chi Nguyen

Food Director - Pamela Clark

Published and Distributed in the United Kingdom by Octopus Publishing Group

Endeavour House

189 Shaftesbury Avenue

London WC2H 8JY

United Kingdom

phone (+44) (0) 207 632 5400; fax (+44) (0) 207 632 5405

info@octopus-publishing.co.uk;

www.octopusbooks.co.uk

Printed by Toppan Printing Co., China

International Foreign Language Rights - Brian Cearnes, ACP Books bcearnes@acpmagazines.com.au

A catalogue record for this book is available from the British Library.

ISBN 978-1-74245-316-3